LANGUAGE ARTS ASSESSMENT

GRADES 1-2

Written by
Concetta Doti Ryan, M.A.

Editor:
Ina Massler Levin, M.A.

Senior Editor:
Sharon Coan, M.S. Ed.

Art Direction:
Elayne Roberts
Darlene Spivak

Product Manager:
Phil Garcia

Imaging:
Rick Chacón

Publishers:
Rachelle Cracchiolo, M.S. Ed.
Mary Dupuy Smith, M.S. Ed.

Teacher Created Materials, Inc.
P.O. Box 1040
Huntington Beach, CA   92647
©1994 Teacher Created Materials, Inc.
Made in U.S.A.

ISBN-1-55734-773-5

Table of Contents _____

Introduction

Recently there has been a revolution in the way we teach language arts. We no longer view reading and writing as isolated tasks to be constantly drilled and tested. Reading and writing are now taught in conjunction with each other and integrated throughout all subject areas. This whole language approach to language arts instruction focuses on literacy development. This method of instruction is not so much concerned with product as it is with process.

As our focus changes from isolated skills to an integrated whole language approach, it becomes necessary to reevaluate our tools of assessment. Do standardized tests, basal tests, and multiple choice writing tests really measure what we as the teachers, the parents, and the students need to know? Essentially what these tests really measure is the student's response to isolated, disconnected questions. To get a more complete picture of the child's progress, a more authentic form of assessment is needed. This needs to be one that is in line with the whole language philosophy and integrated teaching methods. Fortunately, there are now several types of assessment that really look at a child's development in a sophisticated, detailed, authentic manner.

Portfolios were one of the first types of authentic assessment to gain ground. Teachers liked them so much because we felt as if we really had some ownership of them. In other words, there were no specific rules for portfolios. You design the portfolio to match the needs of your students, your classroom, and your assessment procedures.

Recently, other types of authentic assessment are gaining popularity, such as rubrics, conferences, and miscue analysis, just to name a few.

While many teachers acknowledge that diving into authentic assessment is no easy task, it is certainly worth the effort. Fortunately, resource guides such as this one are making it easier for teachers to use more authentic types of assessment in their classrooms

Introduction *(cont.)* _____

This resource guide will help you to implement authentic assessment in your classroom immediately. It provides both theoretical information and ideas for practical application. The types of authentic assessment covered in this resource guide include:

- ✪ Portfolios

- ✪ Inventories and Surveys

- ✪ Anecdotal Records and Observations

- ✪ Logs and Journals

- ✪ Writing Conferences

- ✪ Performance Assessment and Rubrics

- ✪ Miscue Analysis

- ✪ Student Self-Evaluation

- ✪ Parent Evaluation

Literacy Program Evaluation and **Literacy Development Evaluation** are also examined.

Each section begins with "Getting Started." In each you will find the following topics:

Rationale: Theoretical information on that type of authentic assessment.

How to ...: Ideas for how to implement that type of authentic assessment

Using the Forms in this Section: Instructions for using every assessment form included in that section.

For each type of authentic assessment included in this resource guide you will find several blackline forms for immediate use in your classroom. There are also two generic record sheets and bibliography included at the end of the book.

With this extensive resource guide you should feel confident implementing an authentic assessment program in your classroom. It will be worth it to you, to the parents, and most of all, to the students!

Getting Started _____

Rationale

As you make the transition from a more traditional type of assessment to authentic assessment, it may be necessary for you to examine your beliefs about literacy, your classroom environment, your teaching, and student assessment.

Have you ever asked yourself "what is reading" and "what is writing"? In whole language classrooms, these two areas of the curriculum take on a new meaning. Reading is not simply reading a story from the basal and answering several low-level comprehension questions. Instead, it is a process of meaning construction which relies on a student's background knowledge and experience. Writing is no longer simple copying or fill-in-the-blank type activities. Writing now means creating original discourse.

As we examine our beliefs about literacy and what literacy means, we are naturally led to examine the way in which we assess literacy. To establish a method of assessment in your classroom you must first take stock of your personal beliefs about assessment. Once you have defined your beliefs, you can begin to establish goals and procedures for reaching those goals.

How to Evaluate your Literacy Program

There are several items to consider when evaluating your literacy program. One is the literacy environment in your classroom. Is it a print-rich environment that supports and encourages literacy? How are you using print in your classroom? What print materials are readily available to students in your class? Do you model reading and writing for your students? These are some of the questions you may want to ask yourself when evaluating the literacy environment in your classroom.

You also may choose to do a self-evaluation. If we want students to take part in their evaluation, why not become involved in our own? Consider what you are teaching, why you are teaching it, and how you are teaching it. Does it support the literacy environment you seek in your classroom? Then consider how you assess what you teach. Does your assessment tool measure what you need it to measure? By doing some self-analysis, you may become enlightened about your areas of strength and areas that need improvement.

Getting Started *(cont.)* _____

Using the Forms in this Section

Literacy Environment: Classroom Evaluation, Page 7

Evaluate the literacy environment in your classroom by answering "yes" or "no" to some simple questions. Keep in mind the importance of having a print rich environment in a whole language classroom.

Teacher Self-Evaluation, Page 8

It is not always easy to look at our own teaching with a critical eye. However, by doing so we can gain insight into the program we provide for our students. This self-evaluation will ask you to consider the choices you give students, expectations for your students, and your communication skills, among other things.

Personal Beliefs About Assessment, Page 9

Before deciding which types of authentic assessment you want to implement in your classroom, it is important to think about your goals and beliefs about assessment. Use this form to note your personal beliefs and goals for literacy assessment in your classroom. Several example statements are given below.

Evaluation needs to be:
- on-going, informal and formal, clearly defined, and noncompetitive

Evaluation procedures should be:
- based on daily observations, include process and product, and consider parent and student input.

Thematic Unit Evaluation, Page 10

This form is designed to assist you in keeping track of your thematic units, their degree of success, and changes you may wish to make for the following year.

Literacy Environment: Classroom Evaluation

Answer yes or no to each question.

Use of Print in Classroom	Yes	No
Daily messages/schedules/notices	_____	_____
Labels for identification	_____	_____
Interactive bulletin board	_____	_____
Sign in/out sheets	_____	_____
Charts with rules/songs/rhymes/poetry/stories/ instructions/safety procedures	_____	_____
Class calendar	_____	_____

Individual Use of Print	Yes	No
Journals/logs	_____	_____
Students published materials	_____	_____
Access to writing materials	_____	_____
Student mailbox for letter writing	_____	_____

Availability of Printed Material	Yes	No
Variety of literary genres	_____	_____
Nonfiction	_____	_____
Magazines	_____	_____
Comics	_____	_____
Class Books	_____	_____
Student books	_____	_____
Reference materials	_____	_____

Modeling	Yes	No
Read books to students	_____	_____
Read books to self	_____	_____
Write during writing time	_____	_____
Write notes to parents/students/self	_____	_____

Teacher Self-Evaluation

Answer yes or no to each question.

_____ Do I read aloud daily?

_____ Do I provide time for independent reading?

_____ Do I provide time for independent writing?

_____ Do I provide choices for reading?

_____ Do I provide choices for writing?

_____ Do I model reading and writing by doing it myself?

_____ Do I ask open-ended questions?

_____ Do I listen carefully to students' responses?

_____ Do I respect students' responses?

_____ Do I have high expectations for all students?

_____ Do I thoroughly explain evaluation criteria?

_____ Do children in the class feel successful?

_____ Do I comment on students' strengths?

_____ Do I offer suggestions for improvement?

_____ Do I provide time for student interaction and sharing?

_____ Do I encourage students to take responsibility for their learning?

_____ Do I encourage students to self-evaluate?

_____ Do I encourage parents to participate in the evaluation process of their child?

_____ Do I communicate effectively with students?

_____ Do I communicate effectively with parents?

My strengths are: _____

_____

_____

I would like to improve: _____

_____

_____

Literacy Program Evaluation

Personal Beliefs About Assessment

Use this form to note your own personal beliefs and goals for literacy assessment in your classroom. For sample statements, see page 6.

Beliefs Evaluation needs to be:	Goals Evaluation procedures should:

Thematic Unit Evaluation

Unit Title	Unit Description	Date	Degree of Success	Changes for Next Year

Getting Started _____

Rationale

It is important that we look at a child's literacy development over time. Particularly when students are in the lower grades, they change dramatically almost daily. At the very least we should take stock of their development once each quarter so that progress and growth can be maintained and encouraged. This need not be a time consuming process. In fact, for the keen observer completing a developmental checklist can be as easy as 1-2-3.

A checklist is certainly convenient and can give you some good data at a glance; however, it does not always paint a complete picture of the child's development. A narrative form can complement the checklist, providing concrete examples of the development noted in the checklist. The narrative can also help during report card and parent conference time because you can site specific examples.

How to Evaluate Literacy Development

The best way to evaluate literacy development is to become what Yetta Goodman calls a "kidwatcher." (*The Whole Language Catalog*, American School Publishers, 1991). By observing your students on a regular basis you will notice developmental changes and accomplishments. You should take note of reading, writing, listening, and speaking—all four components of language arts.

Children should be "watched" or observed in a variety of settings doing a variety of activities. Observe them during instructional time, play time, reading with partners, and writing stories. Observe students by themselves, with partners, in small groups, and with best friends. Observe students anywhere and anytime you can! As you observe students, make marks on a checklist or brief notes on a narrative form to indicate what you saw at that particular time.

The most comprehensive way to look at literacy development would be to observe students at least once every quarter and complete both a checklist and narrative form. Both a comprehensive checklist and several narrative forms are included in this resource guide. If you do not think you have enough time to do both types of assessment, select the method that you think will work best.

Getting Started *(cont.)*

Using the Forms in this Section

Language Arts Development Checklist, Page 13

This comprehensive four page checklist can be invaluable to you as a "kidwatcher." It is convenient, quick to use, and provides space for reporting on students each quarter. The following categories are included on the checklist: oral language development, listening skills development, reading development, literature response, work patterns, spelling, writing mechanics, and writing. Several blank lines are provided for additional skills you would like to add.

Early Reader Assessment, Page 17

This is another checklist type of assessment form. It asks you to observe the child's print awareness, which is important to the success of early readers. There are three questions on the form as well as room for additional comments.

Assessment of Reading Comprehension: Narrative Form, Page 18

Narrative assessment forms are excellent complements to checklists. This form allows you to score the child's reading ability and provide a narrative of examples based on the child's reading of an unfamiliar book.

Assessment of Writing Development: Narrative Form, Page 19

This is another narrative assessment form, in this case for writing, to complement the checklist. This form asks you to score a writing sample and provide examples based on the child's story. You may wish to attach a photocopy of the child's story to this narrative form for future reference. A completed example of a writing narrative form can be found on page 92 of this book.

Assessment of Oral Language Development: Narrative Form, Page 20

This narrative form asks you to rate the child's oral language development and provide examples of conversation. The form considers both the social context in which the conversation occurred as well as who else participated in the conversation.

Whole Class Language Arts Skill Assessment, Page 21

This checklist includes all the skills mentioned in the three previous narratives, but in a simple checklist form for your convenience.

12

Language Arts Development Checklist

Student's Name _____ Grade _____

Rating Scale: 1 = Rarely Observed
2 = Occasionally Observed
3 = Often Observed

Skill	Quarter			
Oral Language Development	1	2	3	4
Expresses ideas orally with fluency				
Participates in conversation				
Takes turns in conversation				
Participates in small group discussions				
Participates in large group discussions				
Role plays				
Gives directions				
Uses expanded vocabulary				
Explains thinking				
Elaborates responses				
Listening Skills Development	1	2	3	4
Listens attentively:				
in one-to-one interactions				
in small group discussions				
in large group discussions				
to stories read aloud				
Can retell a story				
Comprehends verbal directions				
Recalls information accurately				
Asks questions/seeks clarification				

Language Arts Development Checklist (cont.)

Skill	Quarter			
Reading Development	**1**	**2**	**3**	**4**
Knows letter names				
Knows letter sounds				
Understands directionality:				
top to bottom				
left to right				
turns pages in order				
One-to-one correspondence (finger/word)				
Has basic sight vocabulary				
Uses picture cues				
Uses context to identify meaning				
Makes meaningful substitutions				
Recognizes language patterns				
Monitors reading and self-corrects				
Makes and confirms predictions				
Selects appropriate reading material				
Reads a variety of materials				
Checks books out of school library				
Checks books out of public library				
Literature Response	**1**	**2**	**3**	**4**
Retells story				
Summarizes story				
Sequences story events accurately				
Relates reading to personal experience				
Awareness of story elements:				
setting				
characters				
Discusses story with others				
Gives opinion about the story				
Extends reading through related projects				

Language Arts Development Checklist *(cont.)*

Skill	Quarter			
Work Patterns	**1**	**2**	**3**	**4**
Begins work promptly				
Stays on task				
Shows organization				
Self-directed				
Self-motivated				
Takes risks as a learner				
Works effectively with others				
Is able to self-evaluate				
Spelling	**1**	**2**	**3**	**4**
Uses random letters				
Uses invented spelling				
initial consonant present				
initial and final consonant present				
some vowels present				
Invented spelling makes sense				
High frequency words spelled correctly				
Writing Mechanics	**1**	**2**	**3**	**4**
Prints letter horizontally on page				
Leaves space between words				
Uses age appropriate handwriting				
Uses capital letters:				
for names				
"I"				
at the beginning of a sentence				
Uses correct punctuation				
periods				
question marks				
exclamation points				
Writes in complete sentences				

Language Arts Development Checklist *(cont.)*

Skill	Quarter			
Writing	**1**	**2**	**3**	**4**
Writes 1-5 sentence stories				
Writes 6-10 sentence stories				
Writes 11-20 sentence stories				
Stories have a beginning/middle/end				
Stories develop sequentially				
Uses descriptive words				
Uses story elements				
setting				
character				
Engages promptly in writing task				
Sustains attention to writing task				
Self-selects writing topics				
Shares and discusses writing				
Revises for clarity				
Other	**1**	**2**	**3**	**4**

Early Reader Assessment

Student's Name _____

Age _____   Grade _____   Date _____

Name of book _____

- ☐ This is a new book.
- ☐ The child is somewhat familiar with the book.
- ☐ The child is very familiar with the book.

Ask the child the following questions as he/she looks through the book.

1. Where do you read?

   - ☐ The child points to the words.
   - ☐ The child points to the pictures.
   - ☐ The child moves finger from left to right.
   - ☐ The child moves finger from top to bottom.

2. What do you think this book is about?

   - ☐ The child offers a good prediction.
   - ☐ The child offers a fair prediction.
   - ☐ The child offers no response.

After reading the story to the child ask him/her to retell the story. Then, check all boxes that apply to the child's retelling.

- ☐ The child can retell the story with accuracy.
- ☐ The child retells the story in proper sequence.
- ☐ The child uses book language in retelling.
- ☐ The child is unable to retell the story.

Comments: _____

_____

Assessment of Reading Comprehension: Narrative Form

Student's Name _____

Age _____   Grade _____   Date _____

Use a book the child is unfamiliar with for this comprehension assessment.

Name of book_____

Scoring Scale: 1 = unsuccessful   2 = moderately successful   3 = successful

1. The child can retell the story including all main events.

   Score _____

   Examples/Comments_____

   _____

2. The child can retell the story in chronological order.

   Score _____

   Examples/Comments_____

   _____

3. The child can answer questions about details in the story.

   Score _____

   Examples/Comments_____

   _____

4. The child can define words from the story.

   Score _____

   Examples/Comments_____

   _____

Assessment of Writing Development: Narrative Form

Student's Name _____

Age _____   Grade _____   Date _____

Name of story/assignment _____

Date of writing sample _____

Number of words _____   Number of sentences _____

Scoring Scale: 1 = unsuccessful   2 = moderately successful   3 = successful

1. The story has a beginning, middle and end.

   Score _____

   Examples/Comments _____

   _____

2. The story has a specific setting and characters.

   Score _____

   Examples/Comments _____

   _____

3. The student's knowledge of vocabulary is expanding.

   Score _____

   Examples/Comments _____

   _____

4. There is evidence that the student is moving from invented spelling toward conventional spelling.

   Score _____

   Examples/Comments _____

   _____

Assessment of Oral Language Development: Narrative Form

Student's Name _____

Age _____   Grade _____   Date _____

Context in which the child was observed _____

Names of students child was interacting with _____

Scoring Scale: I = unsuccessful   2 = moderately successful   3 = successful

1. The child participated in a conversation and showed appropriate turn-taking.

   Score _____

   Examples/Comments _____

   _____

2. The child used comprehensible and appropriate speech during the conversation.

   Score _____

   Examples/Comments _____

   _____

3. The child listened and responded appropriately.

   Score _____

   Examples/Comments _____

   _____

4. The child initiated new topics during the conversation.

   Score _____

   Examples/Comments _____

   _____

Whole Class Language Arts Skill Assessment

Name	Tells story with main events	Retells story in chronological order	Knows story details	Defines words in story	Story has beginning, middle, end	Story has setting and characters	Expanding vocabulary	Movement toward conventional spelling	Participates in conversation	Uses appropriate speech	Listens and responds	Initiates new topics

Getting Started _____

Rationale

Recently, there has been a revolution in the way we teach reading. We no longer view reading as an isolated task. Reading and writing are now taught in conjunction with each other and integrated throughout all subject areas. This approach to reading instruction focuses on literacy development and is more concerned with process than product.

As our philosophy and teaching methods of the language arts change, we become aware of the need for a more authentic means of assessment. One such approach to process evaluation is the portfolio. Portfolios represent a philosophy that demands we view assessment as an integral part of instruction. It is an expanded definition of assessment in which a variety of indicators of learning are gathered across many situations. It is a philosophy that honors both the process and the products of learning as well as the active participation of the teacher and the students.

How to Use Portfolios

The first step in beginning to use portfolios in your classroom is determining their purpose. The purpose will depend on the assessment needs in your classroom. Use the questions below to help you establish the purpose for the use of portfolios in your own classroom.

- Will the portfolio be a collection of work or a sample of the student's best work?
- Will the portfolio be passed on to the next teacher?
- Who will select what is included in the portfolio?
- Who will have access to the portfolio?
- How will students be involved with the portfolio?

The next step is to consider where the portfolios will be housed. Depending on your purpose you may or may not want students to have access to the portfolio. If the portfolio is exclusively for your own use, store it in a file cabinet that students do not have access to. On the other hand, if you want students to contribute to their portfolios, keep them in a highly visible place in the classroom. In either case, each student should have a clearly marked file folder to hold the contents of the portfolio. To help establish interest and ownership of the portfolio, allow students to decorate their portfolio folders any way they wish.

Getting Started *(cont.)* _____

Now that you have determined your purpose and set up the portfolio filing system, you must decide on what will be included in the portfolio. The possibilities are endless, including student work samples, self-evaluations, conference reports, and anecdotal records, to name a few. In fact, all of the forms found in this assessment resource guide would be appropriate for the student's portfolio.

The final step in the portfolio process is to decide how you analyze the contents. Having established criteria will help you when report card time rolls around. You can use these criteria to review the contents of the portfolio and determine a formal grade, if your school requires that you give grades. Some schools are moving toward a narrative-type report card in which single grades give way to brief essays regarding student's progress. With this type of grading system, portfolios become an invaluable part of student assessment.

Using the Forms in this Section

Portfolio Writing Sample Cover Sheet, Page 24

If you allow students to take part in the selection process of the portfolio contents, this form is very useful. The students attach the form to the top of a writing samples they have selected for inclusion in the portfolios. On it they write the title of the story selected and why it was selected for the portfolio.

Portfolio Record Keeping, Page 25

This form can help you to keep track of what has been placed in the portfolio. It includes boxes to keep a running tally of the observations, conference notes, and samples that have been collected. By using this form you can be sure that the contents of the portfolio are sufficient to evaluate the student's progress.

Portfolio Content Analysis, Page 26

After all portfolio items have been collected you will want to analyze the student's progress. This narrative form allows you to note the student's strengths and needs for reading, writing, and oral language. This information can then be transferred to the narrative report card or used as concrete data to support report card grades during parent conferences.

Portfolio Writing Sample Cover Sheet

Name: --

Date: --

Title of Story:

_____

_____

I chose this story for my portfolio because:

_____

_____

_____

_____

_____

Portfolio Record Keeping

Student's Name _____   Grade _____

You may wish to note the date in which the item was collected.

Observations	Reading	Writing	Speaking

Conferences	Reading	Writing

Samples	Reading	Writing

Miscellaneous	Reading	Writing
	Speaking	Listening

Portfolio Content Analysis

Student's Name_____

Date_____

Reading Strengths	
Reading Needs	
Writing Strengths	
Writing Needs	
Oral Language Strengths	
Oral Language Needs	

Getting Started _____

Rationale

Interest inventories allow teachers to find out what their students know and what they are interested in knowing. They can also provide basic personal information about students' free time, hobbies, and friends as well as what types of books they like to read and what they like to write about.

Surveys reveal students' attitudes toward subject areas and strategies they employ in different areas of the curriculum. For example, in a reading survey you might ask the child what he does when he comes to a word he does not know. In a writing survey you may ask the child how she decides what to write about.

With both the interest inventory and the survey, you can find out important information about your students and what interests and motivates them. This information can help you significantly when planning curriculum.

One final note regarding interest inventories and surveys. It may be important to stress confidentiality with students. Let them know that this information is for your personal use and will not be made public.

How to Use Inventories and Surveys

Interest inventories can be particularly valuable at the beginning of the year when you are trying to get to know each of your students. The information provided can help you plan thematic units based on the topics your students are interested in.

Surveys are also valuable at the beginning of the year. With this information you can identify which students may need motivational assistance in reading or writing because they do not have a positive attitude toward the subject. You will also know if it is appropriate to introduce a new strategy in reading or writing based on student survey responses. If you use inventories and surveys over time — as at the beginning of the year and then again several months later — you may notice changing attitudes and interests that can again help in planning curriculum. These inventories and surveys can be collected in the student's portfolio if you wish.

Inventories and Surveys

Getting Started *(cont.)* _____

Using the Forms in this Section

Interest Inventory #1, Page 29

When using this inventory with first or second grade students, it is necessary to have an interviewer. This would be an excellent project for parent helpers. Simply give them a copy of the form for each student and have them conduct the interviews. Then, you can review the information at a later, more convenient time. Questions such as #14, "What would you like to learn in school this year?" can be particularly helpful in planning curriculum.

Interest Inventory #2, Page 30

With just five questions, this interest inventory is basic enough so that a first or second grade student can complete it with little or no assistance.

Reading Survey, Page 31

This survey is basic enough for a student to complete with little or no assistance. The first two questions simply ask the student to circle the appropriate response. The last two questions require the student to write an answer. Of particular interest may be the last question in which the student is asked what he/she does when encountering an unfamiliar word.

Writing Survey, Page 32

Again, the student can complete this survey with little or no assistance. It is similar to the reading survey in that the first two questions merely require the student to circle a response. The last two questions require a written answer and can be very enlightening for the teacher. Students are asked how they decide what to write about and also what they like about writing.

Student Survey, Page 33

This blank form can be used to create your own survey on a subject area or topic of your choice. It follows the same format as the reading and writing survey for your convenience. Below is an example of survey questions.

1. How do you feel about dinosaurs?
2. Would you like to learn about dinosaurs?
3. What do you know about dinosaurs?
4. What would you like to know about dinosaurs?

Interest Inventory #1

Student's Name _____

Age _____   Grade _____   Date _____

Name of Interviewer: _____

1. What is your favorite subject in school? _____

2. What is your least favorite subject in school? _____

3. What do you like to do in your free time? _____

4. Who is your best friend? _____

5. What is your favorite sport? _____

6. What is your favorite animal? _____

7. Name something you do very well. _____

8. Name something that makes you angry. _____

9. What is your favorite T.V. show? _____

10. What is your favorite book? _____

11. What is your favorite movie? _____

12. If you could meet a famous person, who would it be? _____

13. Why would you like to meet that person? _____

14. What would you like to learn in school this year? _____

Interest Inventory #2

Name: _____

In school I like to:

_____

At home I like to:

_____

My friend is:

_____

I like to watch:

_____

I like to read:

_____

Reading Survey

Name: _____

1. How do you feel about reading? *(Circle one.)*

2. Is it important to be a good reader? *(Circle one.)*

yes   **not sure**   **no**

3. Write the name of the last book you read.

_____

_____

4. When you come to a word that you do not know, what do you do?

_____

_____

Writing Survey

Name: _____

1. How do you feel about writing? *(Circle one.)*

2. Is it important to be a good writer? *(Circle one.)*

yes   **not sure**   **no**

3. How do you decide what to write about?

_____

_____

4. What do you like about writing?

_____

_____

Student Survey

Name: _____

1.
(Circle one.)

2.
(Circle one.)

yes   **not sure**   **no**

3.
_____

4.
_____

Getting Started _____

Rationale

Anecdotal notes and observations are carefully documented records of certain events, behaviors, and skills. They provide records that you can review independently or share with parents during conference time. When these notes and observations are put together, they tell an on-going story about the student's growth and progress.

Anecdotal records and observations can be objective or interpretive. When using the objective style you simply record what you are seeing as if you were a camera. If you wish to go beyond mere recording, you can try the interpretive style in which you would actually evaluate and comment on your notes and observations. This may be helpful to assist you in recognizing the implications of your observations.

How to Use Anecdotal Records and Observations

Some teachers make a commitment to formally observe each student every few weeks. Others may choose to formally observe a student once a month or once during a single grading period. Your choice will ultimately depend on your available time and class size.

At the beginning of the year it may be necessary to make more general entries as you begin the process of becoming familiar with your students. You may also make notes about certain actions or behaviors to watch for in the future. As you get to know your students throughout the school year, your entries may become more specific or the types of entries may change. For instance at the beginning of the year you may make general notes about students. As the year progresses your notes may become more specific and detailed, focusing on certain concerns you may have.

There are several ways to record anecdotal records and observations. You may wish to keep a single record sheet for each student such as the forms on pages 37, 38, 40, 42, 43, and 45. Or, you may wish to keep a class record sheet to record records and observations such as the forms on pages 39, 41, and 44. Use whatever type form with which you are comfortable.

Getting Started *(cont.)* _____

Using the Forms in this Section

Anecdotal Record Form #1, Page 37

This form can be used to record specific information on a single student. The first three observations are objective, simply asking you to record information. The final question asks you to be interpretive and identify why the behavior was important.

Anecdotal Record Form #2, Page 38

This form can also be used to record information on a single student, but it has space to note several observations. Because you can record several events on this single sheet, it is important to date your observations.

Anecdotal Record Form #3, Page 39

This anecdotal record form can be used to record information about all students in your class. Again, it is important to note the date of your observations. This form is both objective and interpretive in that it asks for a description of the activity and also its possible implications.

Early Reader Observation, Page 40

This form is an observation checklist of basic reading skills for an individual student. You can give a student an unfamiliar book. Then record the skills observed, or simply check them off as you observe the skills in your day-to-day contact with the student. There is space for additional comments at the end of the form for your convenience.

Class Reading Observations, Page 41

This form also serves as a checklist of basic reading skills. There is room to record the information for all students on a single page. All the skills found on the "Early Reader Observation" are included on this form.

Triad Reading Evaluation, Page 42

This is a comprehensive evaluation form that requires participation by the teacher, student, and parent. You must complete the teacher comment portion of the form based on your own observations in the classroom. The students are also asked to give a self-evaluation of their reading behaviors. Parents become involved by making notes of their observations at home. Once all three participants have commented, you can compare the observations and goals indicated. It is important that all parties know that their comments will be read by the teacher as well as the student and parent. Additional copies of this evaluation form are located in the student self-evaluation and parent evaluation sections of this resource guide.

Getting Started *(cont.)* _____

Early Writer Assessment, Page 43

This assessment form serves as a quick way to note an individual student's writing skills. There are three responses for every question: never, seldom, and frequently. These three basic responses make the form extremely easy to use.

Class Writing Observations, Page 44

This form also serves as a checklist of basic writing skills but there is room to record the information for all students on a single page. All of the skills found on the "Early Writer Assessment" are included on this form.

Oral Language Observation, Page 45

Oral language development is very important. This form allows you to record observations about individual student's oral language skills. The form is unique in that it considers both the oral language skill and the social context in which it occurred. This is because the student's oral language may be significantly different in a large group, a small group, or with close friends. There is also room at the bottom of this form to record additional observations of oral language development.

Anecdotal Record Form #1

Student's Name: _____

Date: _____

Subject: _____

Instructional Situation	
Instructional Task	
Behavior Observed	
This behavior was important because	

Anecdotal Record Form #2

Student's Name: _____

Date	Observation	Watch for

Anecdotal Record Form #3

Name	Date	Activity	Implication

Early Reader Observation

Student's Name_____

Age _____   Grade _____   Date _____

Place a check mark next to the comments that reflect the early reading skills of the child you have observed.

_____ Locates front cover of a book.

_____ Locates back cover of a book.

_____ Locates title of a book.

_____ Locates author of a book.

_____ Locates illustrator of a book.

_____ Knows what an author does.

_____ Knows what an illustrator does.

_____ Can find a specific page number.

_____ Reads or moves finger from left to right.

_____ Reads or moves finger from top to bottom.

_____ Reads or "mock" reads.

_____ Is able to read high frequency words.

_____ Can point to a specific word.

_____ Enjoys looking at books.

_____ Listens during story time.

Additional comments: _____

_____

_____

_____

Class Reading Observations

	Locates front cover of a book	Locates back cover of a book	Locates title of a book	Locates author of a book	Locates illustrator of a book	Knows what an author does	Knows what an illusrator does	Can find a specific page number	Reads/moves finger from left to right	Reads/moves finger from top to bottom	Reads or mock reads	Is able to read high frequency words	Can point to a specific word	Enjoys looking at books	Listens during story time

Triad Reading Evaluation

Name: _____

Age: _____ Grade: _____ Date: _____

Interviewer: _____

Student
Parent
Teacher

	Teacher Comment	Student Comment	Parent Comment
Selects books to read			
Reads independently			
Reads at home			
Enjoys reading			
Understands what is read			
Reads a variety of material			
Enjoys listening to stories			

Goals for the year: _____

_____

_____

Early Writer Assessment

Student's Name _____

Age _____   Grade _____   Date _____

Draws pictures:

        never   seldom   frequently

Scribbles and prints "mock" letters:

        never   seldom   frequently

Writes conventional words:

        never   seldom   frequently

Copies printed words:

        never   seldom   frequently

Copies dictated words:

        never   seldom   frequently

Draws and writes in journal:

        never   seldom   frequently

Uses invented spelling:

        never   seldom   frequently

Uses conventional spelling:

        never   seldom   frequently

Asks how to spell words:

        never   seldom   frequently

Class Writing Observations

Student Name	Draws pictures	Scribbles and prints "mock" letters	Writes conventional words	Copies printed words	Copies dictated words	Draws and writes in journal	Uses invented spelling	Uses conventional spelling	Asks how to spell words

44

Oral Language Observation

Student's Name _____

Age _____   Grade _____   Date _____

SOCIAL CONTEXT				
	Pair	**Small Group**	**Close Friends**	**Large Group**
Reading Discussion				
Writer's Workshop				
Dramatic Play				
Free Time				
Playground Time				

OTHER OBSERVATIONS	
Date	Observation

Getting Started _____

The whole language philosophy emphasizes giving students choices in the curriculum. However, if we allow students to select their own books to read and topics to write about, how do we keep track of their progress? Student logs and journals can be excellent ways of charting student work, progress, and attitude.

By having students keep a monthly log of their reading and writing activities, you can be sure that credit is given for all work with a minimum of time and effort. The reading log can be a profile of the reader and answer questions such as what types of books the child enjoys, how much the child is reading, and the level of books chosen for independent reading. The same types of questions can be answered with the writing log. It indicates what types of stories the child writes, how much the child is writing, and whether or not the child ever takes stories through the publication process.

A reading journal is one step beyond the reading log. In the journal the child is asked to respond to the books he/she is reading rather than to keep a list of the titles. By reading the students' journals you can get a good idea not only of their reading comprehension ability, but also of their ability to communicate in writing. The motivation for keeping the journal is the personal response you write back to the student. When teachers and students write back and forth to one another, a more personal relationship can develop. With class sizes constantly increasing, the journal may be the only opportunity for the teacher and student to have a one-to-one correspondence on a regular basis. Students will undoubtedly enjoy this special attention.

How to Use Logs and Journals

When using reading and writing logs students are merely asked to record their activities. This helps both you and students keep a record of their time. Should you find when reviewing the logs that certain students are not as productive as you might like them to be, you can have them complete reading and writing contracts. The contract will help students to plan their time more wisely. Two such contracts are included in this resource book.

Getting Started *(cont.)* _____

As described earlier, reading journals are far more detailed than reading logs. After they read a story on their own or as a class, you may ask the children to respond to the story in their journals. To help you in the evaluation process you may wish to ask students to respond to the following questions:

- What was the story about?
- Do you remember any of the details of the story?
- Where did the story take place?
- Who were the people in the story?
- Did you like the story?

After the child has responded to the story in the journal, it is important that you read the response and write back. This provides the motivation for the student to continue journal writing. After the child has several responses in the journal, you can begin the evaluation process. Read the responses. Then use the "Reading Journal Evaluation" form on page 52 to assist you in the assessment process. One final note — it may be important for you to stress the confidentiality of logs and journals to students. They will often write personal responses and should therefore feel assured that you will be the only one to read them.

Using the Forms in this Section

Monthly Reading Log, Page 49

This form can be used by students to record the reading they do in a one-month period. The form is simple enough that students should be able to complete it with little or no assistance. They are also asked to respond with a check mark to whether or not they liked the book.

Independent Reading Contract, Page 50

If you should find upon review that certain students are not as productive as you might like them to be, you may wish to use this contract. This form will help students to plan their use of time so they can be more productive. Students are asked to report each day on their activities during independent reading time. With this contract you can help students become better time managers.

Getting Started *(cont.)* _____

Bookmark Reading Log, Page 51

This reading log is designed as a bookmark. Students can be encouraged to color it. Each time students open a book the log is right in front of them, which makes it very easy to record their reading time. The bookmark also asks the student to record the date they began the book and the date they finished it, as well as their opinion of the book.

Reading Journal Evaluation, Page 52

If you ask students to keep a journal of their responses to books read, you will need a way to assess these responses. The "Reading Journal Evaluation" is an excellent way of reviewing what the students have written and determining their level of comprehension. The evaluation also considers their ability to communicate in writing, giving this assessment tool a dual purpose.

Monthly Writing Log, Page 53

This form can be used by first and second grade students to record the writing they do in a one-month period. They are also asked to respond with a check mark to what level in the publishing process the writing was taken — such as draft, revision, or publication. This form is simple enough that students should be able to complete it on their own.

Independent Writing Contract, Page 54

If you should find upon review that certain students are not as productive as you might like them to be, you may wish to use this contract. This form will help students to plan their use of time so they can be more productive. Students are asked to report each day on their activities during independent writing time. With this contract you can help students become better time managers.

Monthly Reading Log

Use this form to record all the reading you do in one month.

Name: --

Month: --

Title of Book	Pages	Liked	Disliked

Independent Reading Contract

Name: --

Use this form as a record of your independent reading time.

Monday/Date_____

Tuesday/Date_____

Wednesday/Date_____

Thursday/Date_____

Friday/Date_____

Bookmark Reading Log

Color and cut out a bookmark and use it to record the pages you read each day.

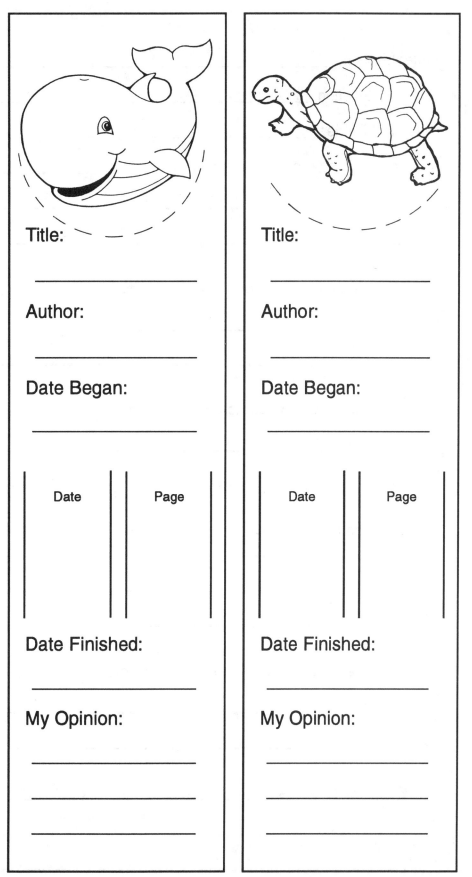

Title:

_____

Author:

_____

Date Began:

_____

Date	Page

Date Finished:

_____

My Opinion:

_____

_____

_____

Title:

_____

Author:

_____

Date Began:

_____

Date	Page

Date Finished:

_____

My Opinion:

_____

_____

_____

Reading Journal Evaluation

Student's Name_____

Date of Evaluation_____

Number of Entries _____

1. Can the reader communicate in writing?_____

    Examples: _____

    _____

2. Can the reader recall details about the story? _____

    Examples: _____

    _____

3. Does the reader appear to understand the story? _____

    Examples: _____

    _____

4. Does the reader appear to understand story elements such as setting, character, and plot?_____

    Examples: _____

    _____

5. Does the reader give an opinion of the story? _____

    Examples: _____

    _____

    Other observations: _____

    _____

    _____

Monthly Writing Log

Use this form to record all the writing you do in one month.

Name: --

Month: ---

Title of Story	Draft	Revised	Published

Independent Writing Contract

Name: ---

Use this form to plan your writing time.

Monday/Date_____
Tuesday/Date_____
Wednesday/Date_____
Thursday/Date_____
Friday/Date_____

Getting Started _____

Rationale

A major component of the writing process has become the writing conference. In the writing conference the student writer reads the story and then talks with a peer or the teacher about what was written. Then the peer or teacher responds to the piece, offering comments and suggestions to the writer for future drafts.

When the student writer is a first or second grade student, options for respondents are more limited because it may be difficult for them to respond to each other. If your own time is limited, you may wish to solicit parent volunteers or upper grade students. Parents are often eager to assist in the classroom, and the writing conference provides them with a very important role. It is important, however, that you take the time to train parents on the conference process. Perhaps this can be arranged as an after school meeting or training session. Upper grade students are often equally as eager to help out with the primary grade classrooms. They can work individually with students to respond to their writing. Try to arrange a convenient time of day with a fourth, fifth, or sixth grade teacher to train your new "assistants."

Although this section focuses on writing conferences only, the section of this resource guide dealing with miscue analysis focuses on the reading conference.

How To Do Writing Conferences

For convenience sake you may wish to schedule a writing workshop time on several days during the week for writing conferences. Because only a few students will be conferencing at any one time, you will need other activities planned for the other students. Perhaps you can direct the rest of the class while the parents and upper grade students conference with individual students.

Getting Started *(cont.)* _____

The first step of the conference is allowing the writer to read the piece on his/her own. The writer should not be interrupted during the reading. Following this reading, the writer should be allowed to talk about the piece or ask questions. Suggest to the parent or peer that they encourage the student through coaching to answer their own questions about the writing. Suggest that the writer guess how to spell something before simply giving the answer. After the writer has had ample time to discuss the writing, the parent or peer can begin to ask questions for clarification. Then, they can offer comments and suggestions to the writer to assist in the revision process. Remind the parent or peer to keep the conference on a positive note as much as possible!

Using the Forms in this Section

Peer Writing Conference, Page 57

This form can be used by either a teacher, parent, or upper grade student to record information about the writing and the conference. It begins on a positive note by asking what was good about the story. Then it asks for clarification and for more details if necessary. At the top of the page the conference steps are listed for convenience.

Student-Teacher Writing Conference, Page 58

This form is more technical in nature and therefore is better suited for the teacher to complete. The form seeks information regarding the student's attitude toward the piece and how he/she reacts to writing miscues while reading the story. For example, what does the student do when he/she reads the story and realizes that a word does not make sense. Does he stop and correct? Does she keep going without correcting? Does the correction show movement toward convention? There is also room at the bottom of the form for additional comments.

Peer Writing Conference

Writer's Name _____

Partner's Name _____

Conference Steps

1. The writer reads the story to a partner.

2. The partner listens very carefully to the story.

3. The writer is then given the opportunity to talk about the writing and to ask questions.

4. The partner comments and offers suggestions to the writer to assist in the revision process.

5. The partner completes the conference form.

Conference Form

1. Tell the writer what you like about the story.

   _____

2. Tell the writer your favorite part of the story.

   _____

   _____

3. I'm confused about:

   _____

   _____

4. Tell me more about:

   _____

   _____

Student-Teacher Writing Conference

Student's Name_____

1. What is the student's attitude toward the piece?

    _____

    _____

    _____

2. What is the student's reaction when he/she sees or hears a miscue in the story?

    _____

    _____

3. Do miscues reveal signs of growth such as movement toward convention?

    _____

    _____

4. Does the student ask questions about conventions?_____

5. Does the student revise or correct language during use? _____

6. What types of changes does the student make when revising or self-correcting?

    _____

    _____

    Additional comments:

    _____

    _____

Getting Started

Rationale

Performance assessment is designed to evaluate students' language behaviors as they are used. Reading performance assessment looks at the reading act in progress and judges the application of comprehension of the text. Performance assessment in writing asks a student to write for a specific audience for a specific purpose. These tasks can then be evaluated using a rubric. A rubric is a set of criteria the student sees prior to engaging in the reading or writing activity. The rubric identifies the qualities the teacher expects to see in a response at several points along a scale. By establishing the criteria prior to the activity, the student clearly knows what is expected in order to receive a specific score. Each score on the rubric is matched to an example of a response.

A rubric can be used in two ways: as an assessment tool and as a teaching tool. When a rubric is used as an assessment tool, it serves as a standard against which a sample of student work can be measured. When a rubric is used as a teaching tool, it provides an example for students to follow.

How to Use Performance Assessment and Rubrics

It is important that the performance task be connected to a piece of real literature. For the reading performance assessment, students should be asked to read a piece of literature in its entirety, complete with all illustrations. The child should then be asked to retell the story. You will match their retelling against the predefined reading rubric you have established for the task. For the writing performance assessment, the student should be asked to respond to a piece of literature. The writing task should be geared toward a specific audience for a specific purpose. Several writing prompt examples can be found on page 62. The student's writing is then scored based on the predefined writing rubric you created. The task and the rubric should be established and discussed clearly with students prior to the activity. The burden of establishing criteria does not always rest upon the teacher, however. You can solicit student's assistance when creating a rubric if you feel they are ready for this responsibility. By assisting in the creation of a rubric, students may become more aware of task expectations and therefore perform better.

Getting Started *(cont.)* _____

Using the Forms in this Guide

Reading Comprehension Rubric, Page 61

This rubric can be used to assess comprehension after students read a story to you or after they have read it independently. Immediately following the reading of the story, ask students to retell the story. Students' responses are then scored against the reading comprehension rubric.

Writing Prompts for Performance Assessment, Page 62

It is important when doing performance assessment that the writing prompt be a response to a real piece of literature. Suggestions for writing prompts based on several popular books are included for your convenience.

Writing Assessment Rubric, Page 63

This rubric can be used to assess writing skill development based on students' responses to the performance assessment prompt. The story is scored based on the criteria established in the rubric. As you collect more and more examples of this type of writing task, you may want to save some as examples of a typical score 3, score 2, and score 1 to share with students.

Oral Language Assessment Rubric, Page 64

This rubric can be used to assess oral language development during a group discussion.

Create a Rubric, Page 65

You can involve students in creating a rubric for any reading, writing, or oral language task. You should begin by clearly defining the task so students know what they will be expected to do. Then, as a class, they can brainstorm the different levels of expectations for the rubric. Certainly students will need a great deal of guidance as they first embark upon creating rubrics. However, in time they can become very good at defining levels of competence, which could in turn help them to become better readers, writers, and speakers.

Reading Comprehension Rubric

Score 3:   *High Pass*

- Student can retell the story in chronological order with details.

- Student has a developed understanding of the text.

- Connections are made between the reader's ideas and experiences and the text.

Score 2:   *Pass*

- Student can retell the story primarily in chronological order with few details.

- Student has a basic understanding of the text.

- Student makes one or two relevant but unsupported comments about the text.

Score 1:   *Needs Assistance*

- Student can retell general ideas about the story with no details.

- Student shows little evidence of meaning construction.

- Student makes irrelevant comments relating to the text.

Score O: Student did not understand the story.

Writing Prompts for Performance Assessment

Alexander and the Wind-Up Mouse by Leo Lionni
Stop reading at the end of page 17.

Writing Prompt: Now that Alexander knows that Willy is being thrown away, do you think he still wants to be a wind-up mouse? Write a letter from Willy to Alexander trying to convince him not to become a wind-up mouse.

Imogene's Antlers by David Small
Read the story in its entirety.

Writing Prompt: Write a new story with yourself as the main character. Imagine that you had grown an elephant's trunk instead of antlers. Then, write the story of what your day was like with the elephant trunk on your face.

Strega Nona Meets Her Match by Tomie dePaola
Stop reading at the end of page 12.

Writing Prompt: Strega Nona has met her match! Help her to get her customers back! Write a speech for Strega Nona to give to her customers to try to get them to come back to her.

Wilfred Gordon McDonald Partridge by Mem Fox
Stop reading at the end of page 13.

Writing Prompt: Wilfred Gordon McDonald Partridge has asked many people what a memory is. Imagine that he asked you what you think a memory is. Write a response to Wilfred Gordon about your favorite memory.

Where the Wild Things Are by Maurice Sendak
Read the book in its entirety.

Writing Prompt: Max was disrespectful to his mother and so she sent him to his room. What do you think Max's punishment should have been for talking back to his mother? Write a punishment suggestion to give to Max's mom.

Writing Assessment Rubric

Score 3: *High Pass*

- Student responds to prompt.

- Student writes more than one complete sentence with correct capitalization and punctuation.

- Student primarily uses conventional spelling.

- Invented spelling is phonetic.

Score 2: *Pass*

- Student responds to prompt.

- Student expresses complete thoughts, not necessarily in complete sentences.

- Student attempts to spell with beginning and ending consonants.

Score 1: *Needs Assistance*

- Student may not respond to prompt.

- Student expresses self in a way that inhibits understanding.

- Student does not demonstrate knowledge of sound/symbol relationships.

Score O: No response.

Oral Language Assessment Rubric

Score 3:   *High Pass*

- Student made relevant comments and suggestions during the discussion.

- Student took on a leadership role and encouraged the discussion.

- Student used appropriate turn-taking skills.

Score 2:   *Pass*

- Student made relevant comments during the discussion.

- Student actively participated in the discussion.

- Student primarily used appropriate turn-taking skills.

Score 1:   *Needs Assistance*

- Student made irrelevant comments during the discussion.

- Student participated in the discussion, but was easily distracted.

- Student interrupted while others were speaking.

Score O: Child did not speak at all during discussion.

Create a Rubric

Score 3:   *High Pass*

Score 2:   *Pass*

Score 1:   *Needs Assistance*

Score O: *No response.*

Getting Started _____

Rationale

Miscue analysis is a type of reading assessment that considers both the reading of the text and the retelling of the story as equally important. In the past we may have determined children's reading ability based on how well they read out loud, regardless of comprehension. Miscue analysis takes reading assessment to a much higher level, a level more consistent with the whole language philosophy. It is therefore no surprise that Ken Goodman, often noted as the "father of whole language," also developed the miscue analysis procedure.

A miscue is an unexpected response by a reader to the printed text. A miscue provides a window into the strategies and cueing systems (semantic, syntactic, and grapho-phonic) children use when reading an unknown text. Definitions for each of the cueing systems are noted below. Miscue analysis is based on the notion that every reading response is based on a reader's knowledge of language, experiences, and printed text. By analyzing the miscues, you can determine students' confirming and predicting reading skills and their control of the cueing systems. Control of all three cueing systems leads to effective meaning construction and comprehension.

Cueing Systems

- **Semantic:** meaning cues from the sentence
- **Syntactic:** grammatical cues such as word order
- **Grapho-phonic:** correspondence between letters and sounds

---

Getting Started *(cont.)*

How to do a Miscue Analysis

The first step in the miscue process is to select a book for the child to read that you would consider to be slightly challenging. The child must be given the entire text complete with illustrations. Anything less would not provide the child with the complete context to construct meaning of the text and is therefore not fair to the reader.

In order to do a miscue analysis, you will need a photocopy of the entire text the student is reading. Have several spaces between lines so that you can write the miscues in as the child reads. You can use a basic marking system as shown below, or you can simply use another marking system you feel comfortable with. Whatever you choose, the procedure is to mark the miscue as the child is reading the text to you by listening carefully to the reading. A sample of a miscue marking can be found on page 92. You may elect to tape record the child's reading if you are worried that you may not be able to catch everything as the child reads. This is fairly common when you are beginning to do miscue analyses. The miscues noted on your copy of the text can later be transferred to "Miscue Analysis Form: Part A" located on page 69 for future analysis.

Marking System

- Substitutions—Write them directly above the expected response.

  amazon
  ~~amazing~~

- Omissions—Circle the word that is omitted.

  (breakfast)

- Insertions—Indicate the insertion in the appropriate place in the text with a caret (^) and note what word was substituted.

  his
  For/breakfast

- Repeated Words—Show them by drawing a line under the word the number of times the child repeats the word.

  dozen

After all miscues have been recorded, you can begin the retelling portion of the miscue analysis. "Miscue Analysis Form: Part A," "Miscue Analysis Form: Part B," and "Miscue Analysis Form: Part C" will all be completed when you have finished your interaction with the child.

Getting Started *(cont.)* _____

In the retelling portion of the miscue procedure, you ask the student to retell the story. The retelling is the most important aspect of the miscue analysis. The focus of this procedure is whether or not a child is able to comprehend the text. If you are a miscue novice, it may be easier for you to have a few books that you use regularly when doing miscue analyses. It is important to remember that during the retelling you should never interrupt and offer coaching only to get more information from the child. Statements such as "Can you tell me more about...?" or "Can you explain....?" are good coaching questions. You should make notes during the retelling or tape record the session for later review. After the retelling, you can analyze the miscues by using pages 69 through 71. You should also categorize statements made by the student during the retelling according to the prompts on page 72. Although miscue analysis is a time consuming process, there is no doubt that it provides invaluable information about a child's reading ability.

Using the Forms in this Section

Miscue Analysis Form: Part A, Page 69

Once you have recorded a child's miscues on your copy of the text, they can be transferred to this form. You should note the actual text as well as the child's miscue. A completed sample of this form can be found on page 92.

Miscue Analysis Form: Part B, Page 70

Using the information from "Part A" the miscues can be analyzed and then notes can be made on this form. A completed sample of this form can be found on page 92.

Miscue Analysis Form: Part C, Page 71

Based on the notes you recorded in "Part B" you can make some evaluations about which cueing systems the reader uses. This will help you to determine if the child is relying on one system rather than using all systems simultaneously. A completed sample of this form can be found on page 92.

Miscue Analysis Form: Part D, Page 72

This form is to be used following the retelling. Statements made by a student during the retelling are coded onto this form. By evaluating the information on this form, you can determine if a child is able to construct the meaning of the text and whether or not he/she has a grasp of basic story elements. A completed sample of this form can be found on page 92.

Miscue Analysis Form: Part A

Student's Name _____

Age _____   Grade _____   Date _____

Text	Reader

Miscue Analysis Form: Part B

Student's Name _____

Age _____   Grade _____   Date _____

Title of Book _____

1. Did the miscues go with the preceding text? _____

2. Did the miscues go with the following text? _____

3. Did the miscues leave the essential meaning of the sentence intact?

    _____

4. Did the miscues leave the essential meaning of the story intact?

    _____

5. Were the miscues corrected? _____

6. Were the miscues appropriate substitutions? _____

7. Did the miscues have graphic similarity? _____

8. Did the miscues have sound similarity? _____

9. Did the miscues have grammatical similarity? _____

10. Are the miscues grammatically sensible? _____

    Other Observations:

    _____

    _____

    _____

    _____

    _____

Miscue Analysis Form: Part C

Student's Name _____

Age _____   Grade _____   Date _____

Title of Book _____

1. Does the student use context clues? _____

    Examples: _____

    _____

2. Does the student use picture clues? _____

    Examples: _____

    _____

3. Does the student use phonetic clues? _____

    Examples: _____

    _____

4. Does the student self-correct? _____

    Examples: _____

    _____

5. Does the student make appropriate substitutions? _____

    Examples: _____

    _____

6. Other observations:

    _____

Miscue Analysis Form: Part D

Student's Name _____

Age _____   Grade _____   Date _____

Title of Book _____

Character Statements:

Setting Statements:

Plot Statements:

Misconceptions:

Additional Comments:

_____

_____

_____

Getting Started _____

Rationale

In whole language classrooms, learning is seen as a joint venture between the teacher and the student. Naturally, then, the responsibility for evaluation should also be shared between teacher and student. Self-evaluation makes students aware of their own learning, progress, and growth throughout the school year. It is an indispensable part of any learning and assessment program that strives to have students take responsibility for their own learning. Self-evaluation requires reflection about academic work and attitude. Perhaps difficulty with a certain subject has nothing to do with content, and rather everything to do with motivation. By taking time to reflect, students can determine where their strengths and weaknesses lie and how to pinpoint what exactly is causing the difficulty.

How to use Student Self-Evaluation

We can not expect students to jump right into self-evaluation, they must be trained. Traditionally, students do the work and wait for the teacher to return it with a grade on top. Evaluating your own work is not easy and taking the responsibility for doing so is a challenge. The forms in this resource guide will help students to gradually become engaged in the self-evaluation process. They are asked to reflect on their academic achievement and their attitude, both important components of learning.

It is important for you to stress confidentiality with student self-evaluations. Students may be reluctant to self-report and self-assess accurately if they fear their answers will be made public.

Using the Forms in this Section

Today I Learned..., Page 76

How many times do students arrive home faced with the question "What did you learn in school today?" If students constantly answer "Oh, nothing," parents may wonder exactly what we are doing in our classrooms. By having students complete this form on a daily basis they are forced to reflect on their learning for the day. When they go home they will have plenty to discuss!

Getting Started *(cont.)* _____

Assignment Self-Evaluation, Page 77

This form asks students to evaluate a specific assignment. Students are asked how they feel about the assignment, what they did best, and where they need to improve. The form is easy enough for first or second graders to complete on their own. Notes students make regarding what needs improvement can be used for future self-evaluations and reflections. If you would like students to write their feelings, cover the faces in question one before reproducing.

Reading Reflections, Page 78

Students need to reflect on their attitudes toward reading. This form asks students not only to reflect on their attitudes, but also how the attitudes change through the school year. This form is simple enough for students to complete on their own. If you would like students to write their feelings, cover the faces in questions one and two before reproducing.

Reading Concepts Self-Evaluation, Page 79

This form requires that an interviewer work with the student. As mentioned in earlier sections of this resource guide, parents and upper grade students can be excellent interviewers for your students. This self-evaluation requires that students consider their attitudes toward reading and their reading activities beyond the classroom situation.

Triad Reading Evaluation, Page 80

This is the second copy of this evaluation form which considers comments from teachers, students, and parents. Additional copies can be found in the Anecdotal Record and Observation section and Parent Evaluation section. Students, with the help of an interviewer, are asked to respond to basic questions about their reading habits. You can compare your own comments to those of the students and parents as well.

Spelling Self-Evaluation, Page 81

This basic form asks students to consider their progress in spelling. This form is simple enough for students to complete on their own. If you would like students to write their feelings, cover the faces in question one before reproducing.

Getting Started *(cont.)* _____

Writing Reflections, Page 82

Students need to reflect on their writing ability. They should consider how they are improving and what they already do very well. This form will help students to evaluate their writing progress. The form is simple enough for students to complete on their own. If you would like students to write their feelings, cover the faces in question one before reproducing.

Writing Concepts Self-Evaluation, Page 83

This form requires that an interviewer work with the student. As mentioned in earlier sections of this resource guide, parents and upper grade students could be excellent interviewers for your students. This self-evaluation requires that students consider their attitudes toward writing and their writing activities beyond the classroom situation.

Self-Evaluation Editing Checklist, Page 84

Prior to working with a partner in a writing workshop situation students should be encouraged to evaluate their own piece of writing. This form asks students to read the story to themselves, and to check capitalization and punctuation. They are also asked to note words they corrected and those of which they are still unsure. By completing this form prior to the writing workshop, students will be better prepared for the conference.

Today I learned.....

Name: _____

Date: _____

Today at school I learned.........

1. _____

2. _____

3. _____

Assignment Self-Evaluation

Name: _____

Assignment: _____

1. How do you feel about this assignment? *(Circle one.)*

2. What did you do best on this assignment?

_____

_____

3. What could you improve on this assignment?

_____

_____

Reading Reflections

Name: _____

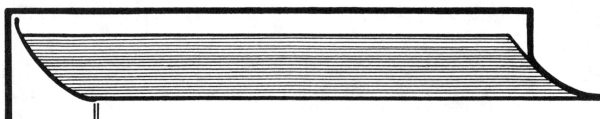

1. When I read at the beginning of the year, I felt....

(Circle one.)

happy   **not sure**   **sad**

2. Now when I read I feel.... *(Circle one.)*

happy   **not sure**   **sad**

3. My reading has improved because....

_____

- -

_____

4. I am really proud of....

_____

- -

_____

5. My favorite book is.....

_____

- -

_____

Reading Concepts Self-Evaluation

Student's Name_____

Age _____   Grade _____   Date _____

Name of Interviewer: _____

1. Do you know how to read? _____

2. How did you learn to read? _____

3. Do you like to read?_____

4. What do you read?_____

5. Is reading easy or hard? _____

6. Is learning to read important? _____

   Why? _____

7. Why do people read?_____

8. Do you read at home? _____

9. Why do you read at home? _____

10. What do you read at home? _____

11. Do the people in your family read? _____

12. What do they read?_____

13. Do they ever read to you? _____

14. What do they read to you? _____

15. Where do they read to you? _____

16. When do they read to you?_____

17. What do you look at while you are being read to? _____

18. Do you ever go to the public library? _____

19. Do you check out books? _____

20. What types of books do you check out?_____

21. Name some of your favorite books. _____

22. Do you have any comments about reading? _____

_____

Student Self-Evaluation

Triad Reading Evaluation

Name: _____

Age: _____ Grade: _____ Date: _____

Interviewer: _____

Student

Parent

Teacher

	Teacher Comment	Student Comment	Parent Comment
Selects books to read			
Reads independently			
Reads at home			
Enjoys reading			
Understands what is read			
Reads a variety of material			
Enjoys listening to stories			

Goals for the year:

_____

- -

_____

#773 Language Arts Assessment: 1-2   80   *©1994 Teacher Created Materials, Inc.*

Spelling Self-Evaluation

Name: _____

1. This is how I feel about my progress in spelling: *(Circle one.)*

   happy   not sure   sad

2. Here are some new words I have learned how to spell:

   _____

   _____

3. I have trouble spelling:

   _____

   _____

4. When I don't know how to spell a word, I usually....

   _____ ask the teacher.

   _____ ask a friend.

   _____ make a guess.

   _____ sound it out.

   _____ look in the dictionary.

Writing Reflections

Name: _____

1. After reading my story I feel.... *(Circle one.)*

happy   not sure   sad

2. I have improved in:

_____ writing complete sentences.

_____ using capital letters.

_____ using correct punctuation.

_____ spelling.

_____ telling a story.

_____ handwriting.

3. I am most proud of:

_____

_____

_____

4. Next time I write I will try to:

_____

_____

_____

Writing Concepts Self-Evaluation

Student's Name _____

Age _____   Grade _____   Date _____

Name of Interviewer: _____

1. Do you know how to write stories? _____
2. How did you learn to write? _____
3. Write something for me.
4. Tell me what you wrote.
5. Do you like to write? _____
6. Is writing easy or hard? _____
7. When do you write? _____
8. What do you write about? _____
9. How do you decide what to write about? _____
10. Is writing important? _____
    Why? _____
11. Do you ever write at home? _____
12. What do you write at home? _____
13. Do the people in your family write? _____
14. What do they write? _____
15. Do you ever draw pictures to go with your writing? _____
16. Draw a picture to go with what you wrote for me.
17. Tell me about the drawing.
18. What made you draw this picture to go with your story? _____
19. Do you have any other comments about writing? _____

    _____

    _____

    _____

    _____

Self-Evaluation Editing Checklist

Name: _____

_____ I read the story to myself and it makes sense.

_____ I read the story to a friend.

_____ Every sentence begins with a capital letter.

_____ Every sentence ends with a punctuation mark.

_____ I checked my spelling.

These are the words I corrected:

_____

_____

_____

_____

_____

These are the words I am unsure about:

_____

_____

_____

_____

_____

Getting Started _____

Rationale

We take great pains to keep the parents of our students informed regarding student progress and classroom activities. However, the whole language philosophy asks that we go one step beyond mere distribution of information. Parents can be invited to take part in the evaluation of the child's growth and progress. By involving parents the assessment cycle is complete because all three participants in the child's education — the teacher, child, and parent— are involved in evaluation.

Parent responses on evaluation forms can often give you great insight to the ways literacy is viewed and valued at the child's home. In addition, by asking parents to take a more active role in evaluation, they will naturally become more involved in the child's homework. Home reading and writing logs can help parents to realize when their child is spending too much time playing or watching T.V. rather than engaging in literacy activities such as reading or writing.

Another benefit of parent evaluation is clearly seen at parent conference time. Parents are better informed and better able to discuss their child's progress with you. Now the conference is a two way conversation between teacher and parent rather than a one way monologue performed by the teacher directed at the parent. This can greatly reduce the possible stress of parent-teacher conference time for all parties involved.

How to Use Parent Evaluations

Parents, like students, need to be adequately trained in how to evaluate. It may be well worth your time to schedule parent training sessions after school. In this way, parents can be well informed about the process. Although it will take time to plan such training sessions, in the long run you will get more and better information on the parent response forms if they are properly trained.

Getting Started *(cont.)* _____

Using the Forms in this Section:

Parent Observation Form, Page 87

This observation form asks parents to evaluate their children on basic items and tasks based on parent observations at home. Reading, writing, and oral language skills are all considered. Room for parent questions and comments has been provided on the form.

Parent Questionnaire, Page 88

It is important for parents to consider their children's strengths and weaknesses in the classroom. They should also consider what goals they have for their children so they can help their children to achieve them. This form will help parents direct the present and future of their children's education. Space for parents to write additional comments is provided.

Triad Reading Evaluation, Page 89

This is the final copy of this evaluation form which asks teacher, student, and parent to evaluate the same categories. After parents have returned their comments, you can compare them to your responses, as well as the students'. Additional copies of this form can be found in the Anecdotal Records and Observations section and Student Self-Evaluation section.

Home Reading Log, Page 90

Students, with the help of their parents, can keep track of the books they read at home as well as the time they spend reading. As mentioned earlier, this log may help parents to realize when their children are spending too much time on play and too little time on literacy.

Home Writing Log, Page 91

Students, with the help of parents, can keep track of the writing they do at home as well as how much time they spend writing. As with the reading log, the writing log can help parents to realize whether their children are spending enough time on writing activities or not.

Parent Observation Form

Student's Name _____

Name of parent completing form:_____

Please place a check under the appropriate response.

	Usually	**Sometimes**	**Rarely**
Speaks clearly			
Follows directions			
Enjoys being read to			
Reads to me			
Enjoys talking about books			
Checks out books from school and public library			
Draws pictures and write letters			
Uses invented spelling			
Uses conventional spelling			
Enjoys talking about writing			

Questions I have: _____

_____

_____

_____

Parent Questionnaire

Student's Name _____

Age _____ Grade _____ Date _____

Name of adult completing form: _____

1. What is going well for your child this year?

   _____

   _____

   _____

2. What progress has your child made since the beginning of the school year?

   _____

   _____

   _____

3. Do you have any concerns about your child?

   _____

   _____

   _____

4. Do you have any suggestions for working with your child?

   _____

   _____

   _____

5. What are your goals for your child this school year?

   _____

   _____

   _____

   Additional Comments:

   _____

   _____

Thank you for your time!

Triad Reading Evaluation

Student's name: _____

Name of parent completing form: _____

Please complete the parent comment portion of this reading
evaluation form. Then have your child return it to the teacher.

Student
Parent
Teacher

	Teacher Comment	Student Comment	Parent Comment
Selects books to read			
Reads independently			
Reads at home			
Enjoys reading			
Understands what is read			
Reads a variety of material			
Enjoys listening to stories			

Goals for the year: _____

_____

Home Reading Log

Student's Name _____

Name of parent completing form: _____

Please record the time your child spends reading at home.

Date	Title of Book	Pages	Time Start	Time Stop

Thanks for your time!

Home Writing Log

Student's Name _____

Name of parent completing form: _____

Date	Title of Book	Pages	Time Start	Time Stop

Thanks for your time!

Sample Completed Forms

Page 19

Literacy Development Evaluation

Assessment of Writing Development:
Narrative Form

Miscue for: *Paul Bunyan*

Student's Name ___Sally Barber___

A story is told about an amazing baby who at

amazon

two weeks old weighed more than one

hundred pounds. For breakfast every morning

is

he ate five dozen eggs, ten sacks of potatoes,

bowl

and a half barrel of mush. The baby's

strangest feature was his curly black beard. It

bird

was so big and bushy his poor mother had to

climb
comb it for him every day.

©1994 Teacher Created Materials, Inc.

	Student's Name ___Liza Bellwood___
Age __6__ Grade __1__	Date __4/22/94__

Name of story/assignment __My New Dog__
Date of writing sample __4/20/94__
Number of words __30__   Number of sentences __5__

Scoring Scale: 1 = unsuccessful   2 = moderately successful   3 = successful

1. The story has a beginning, middle and end.
   Score ___3___
   Examples/Comments

2. The story has a specific setting and characters.
   Score ___3___
   Examples/Comments

3. The student's knowledge of vocabulary is expanding.
   Score ___2___
   Examples/Comments

4. There is evidence that the student is moving from invented spelling toward conventional spelling.
   Score ___2___
   Examples/Comments

©1994 Teacher Created Materials, Inc.

Page 70

Miscue Analysis

Miscue Analysis Form: Part B

	Student's Name ___Paul Bunyan___
Age __8__ Grade __2__	Date __4-20-94__

Title of Book ___Paul Bunyan___

1. Did the miscues go with the preceding text?
2. Did the miscues go with the following text?
3. Did the miscues leave the essential meaning of the sentence intact?
4. Did the miscues leave the essential meaning of the story intact?
5. Were the miscues corrected?
6. Were the miscues appropriate substitutions?
7. Did the miscues have graphic similarity?
8. Did the miscues have sound similarity?
9. Did the miscues have sound similarity?
10. Are the miscues grammatically sensible?

Other Observations:

©1994 Teacher Created Materials, Inc.

Page 71

Miscue Analysis

Miscue Analysis Form: Part C

	Student's Name ___Sally Barber___
Age __8__ Grade __2__	Date __4-20-94__

Title of Book ___Paul Bunyan___

1. Does the student use context clues?
   Examples:
2. Does the student use picture clues?
   Examples:
3. Does the student use phonetic clues?
   Examples:
4. Does the student self-correct?
   Examples:
5. Does the student make appropriate substitutions?
   Examples:
6. Other observations:

©1994 Teacher Created Materials, Inc.

Page 69

Miscue Analysis

Miscue Analysis Form: Part A

	Student's Name ___Sally Barber___
Age __8__ Grade __2__	Date __4/20/94__

Text	Reader
① a story is told about	① a story is told about
② an amazing baby	② an amazon baby
③ one hundred pounds	③ a hundred pounds
④ for breakfast	④ for his breakfast
⑤ five dozen eggs	⑤ five dozen eggs
⑥ half barrel of mush	⑥ half bowl of mush
⑦ curly black beard	⑦ curly black bird
⑧ had to comb it	⑧ had to climb it

©1994 Teacher Created Materials, Inc.

Page 72

Miscue Analysis

Miscue Analysis Form: Part D

	Student's Name ___Sally Barber___
Age __8__ Grade __2__	Date __4-20-94__

Title of Book ___Paul Bunyan___

Character Statements:

Setting Statements:

Plot Statements:

Misconceptions:

Additional Comments:

©1994 Teacher Created Materials, Inc.

Award

Congratulations

to

_____

For Outstanding Achievement in

_____

_____

_____   _____
Teacher Signature   *Date*

Generic Record Sheet A

94

Generic Record Sheet B

	Monday	Tuesday	Wednesday	Thursday	Friday	Monday	Tuesday	Wednesday	Thursday	Friday	Monday	Tuesday	Wednesday	Thursday	Friday

Language Arts Assessment Bibliography

Anthony, Robert J., Terry D. Johnson, Norma I. Mickelson, and Alison Preece. *Evaluating Literacy: A Perspective for Change.* Heinemann, 1991

Barrs, Myra, Sue Ellis, Hilary Hester, and Anne Thomas. *The Primary Language Record.* Heinemann, 1988

Gentry, J. Richard. *Spel...is a Four Letter Word.* Scholastic, 1987

Goodman, Kenneth. *What's Whole in Whole Language.* Scholastic, 1986

Goodman, Kenneth S., Lois Bridges Bird, and Yetta Goodman. *The Whole Language Catalog Supplement on Authentic Assessment.* Macmillan, 1992

Jasmine, Julia. *Portfolio Assessment for Your Whole Language Classroom.* Teacher Created Materials, 1992

Jasmine, Julia. *Portfolios and Other Assessments.* Teacher Created Materials, 1993

Kamii, Constance, Maryann Manning, and Gary Manning (Eds.). *Early Literacy: A Constructivist Foundation for Whole Language.* National Education Association, 1991

Routman, Regie. *Transitions.* Heinemann, 1988

Routman, Regie. *Invitations.* Heinemann, 1991

Tierney, Robert J., Mark A. Carter, and Laura E. Desai. *Portfolio Assessment in the Reading-Writing Classroom.* Christopher Gordon Publishers. 1991

Valencia, Sheila W., Elfrieds H. Hiebert, and Peter P. Afflerbach. *Authentic Reading Assessment: Practices and Possibilities.* International Reading Association, 1994